Evening **Express**

Aberdeen
Moments in Time

with special
Union Street feature

Evening **Express**

Aberdeen
Moments in Time

with special
Union Street feature

Raymond Anderson

The Breedon Books
Publishing Company
Derby

First published in Great Britain by
The Breedon Books Publishing Company Limited
Breedon House, 44 Friar Gate, Derby, DE1 1DA.
1996

ISBN 1 85983 070 6

Printed and bound by Butler & Tanner Ltd., Selwood Printing
Works, Caxton Road, Frome, Somerset.

Colour separations by Colour Services, Wigston, Leicester.

Jackets printed by Lawrence-Allen, Weston-super-Mare, Avon.

Contents

Introduction

IT was with some trepidation that I approached doing a second compilation of historic Aberdeen photographs. Could the success of the first book be repeated? Were there sufficient different photographs in the Aberdeen Journals library?

The second question was quickly answered because Duncan Smith, Ken Mackay and Bob Stewart had made good progress in their ongoing task of filing and indexing the historic Journals photographs.

With that as a solid base to start from the spur to try again came from the reactions of readers to the first book. That fairly disparate collection of images had obviously stirred memories and evoked times that meant much to many Aberdonians.

All manner of finds were made in those photographs — unknown to me an acquaintance stood barely seen behind a window in one of the wartime scenes. Relatives identified people long since departed our shores, and a friend pointed out that my wife was in one crowd scene. That is the fun of a book like this. Who knows what the photographs will reveal on close examination?

The popularity of the first book says much for Aberdonians' sense of their own identity and love of their city. *Images of Aberdeen* was the best seller of the series of some 40 books, far outselling editions on cities like Edinburgh, Manchester and even London.

This year it has been necessary to shift the focus. The wartime photographs, for instance, have been well used over the years and there is no complete section on those momentous times in this book. That has, however, allowed me the chance to give more space to other aspects of this city of ours — like the airport which we take for granted today, but has a fascinating history. I'm glad to be able to give it the prominence it deserves.

Education and the fine schools built in Aberdeen for five decades after 1872 have a special place in this book. These sturdy granite buildings remain a testimony to the canny Aberdonian habit of investing in the future.

That special sense of place is part of the distinctive Aberdeen character which has, to a great extent, remained intact over the years. I hope that some part of that character is caught in these photographs which celebrate a remarkable city and its remarkable citizens.

Raymond Anderson
Aberdeen
August, 1996

Schooldays

Ashley Road School which opened its doors on December 3, 1888, and had a first-year roll of 1,200. In those days youngsters started school at five and left at 12.

Broomhill School, an imposing tribute to the importance of education at the turn of the century.

Commerce Street School, a haven of learning in a bustling part of the city.

Causewayend School, and some of the pupils.

Ferryhill School, a sedate playtime for a few pupils.

Frederick Street School in 1907, two years after it opened. Separate boys' and girls' playgrounds were divided by a spiked fence.

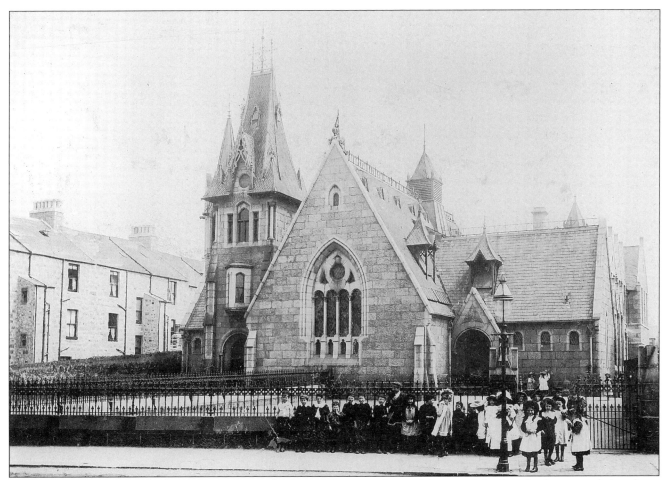

Holburn Street School, showing girls in their cotton smocks and boys with the cloth caps of the day.

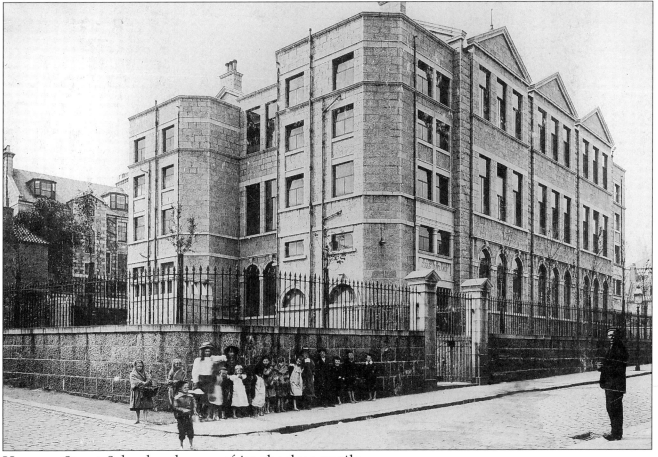

Hanover Street School and some of its shoeless pupils.

Kittybrewster School, with a fine surrounding garden.

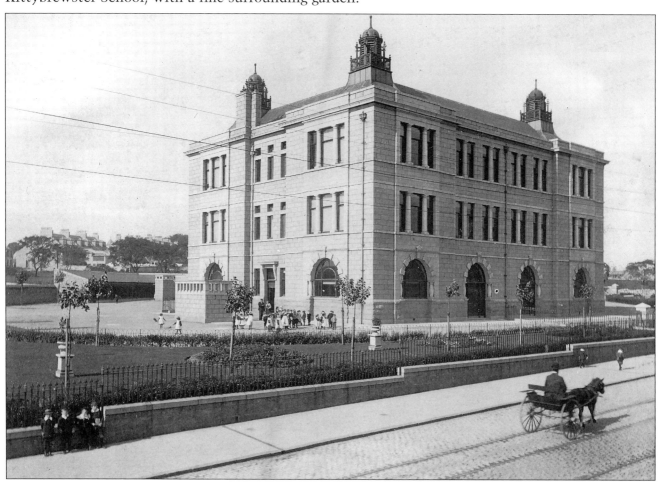

Another view of Kittybrewster School showing the few houses around it in the early 1900s.

Mile End School, an imposing beginning-of-the-century building when today's mature trees were mere striplings.

Old Aberdeen School, a grand building of learning.

Ruthrieston, another
good example of
1900's architecture
with an impressive
double stairway.

St Paul Street School
from Loch Street.

Skene Square School ready to serve the surrounding area.

The old Grammar School which was completed in 1758 and survived until 1864.

The impressive replacement Grammar School , the young trees showing the newness of the development

Robert Gordon's College, a classic design for learning.

York
Street
School,
cloth
caps and
boots ...
but only
for
some.

Torry
Nursery,
a scene
from the
1940s.

Outdoor lessons for evacuees to Deeside in September, 1939.

Kirkhill Primary School at Kincorth, the shape of schooling in 1957.

An historic
scene, the
opening of
the new
Marischal
College by
King
Edward
V11 in
1906.

Marischal
College,
the early
buildings
were added
to in 1906.

Some of the first women students at Aberdeen University in 1900.

Aberdeen decked out in decorations for the Quarter-Centenary of Aberdeen University and the opening of Marischal College by Edward VII in 1906. The lavish celebrations were delayed 11 years for the State Visit of the King and Queen.

In the early 1900s rectorial elections and addresses were often rowdy affairs. Here a carriage for Prime Minister H.H.Asquith is wrecked by hundreds of students in 1910 after his rectorial address. Mr Asquith looked on amused, but declined to take his seat in the landau which eventually ended in Aberdeen harbour.

A dignified protest in 1951 during the campaign to have the black singer Paul Robeson elected rector of Aberdeen University.

Police batons drawn during rectorial election riots in 1955.

The snowball rector. John Bannerman, Scots rugby international, Liberal leader and Gaelic scholar, is carried shoulder high to the Kirkgate Bar after his election in 1958.

Rival supporters pelt each other with flour, soot — and anything else that comes to hand — during the traditional rectorial battle in the Marischal College quad.

New rector Sir Roderick McGregor has a celebratory half-pint in the Kirkgate Bar in 1955.

Naturalist Peter Scott is rushed to the Kirkgate Bar in 1961, after being installed as rector.

Rowdy celebrations in the Kirkgate Bar as newly-installed rector Sir John Hunt oversees the 1964 victory drinks.

Torcher Night 1978 as the students stream on to the streets of Aberdeen to get as much cash as possible for their charities campaign.

The Torcher procession leaves
Marischal College in 1969.

The chase is on with Britannia in
pursuit of charity pennies in 1968.

Life of Leisure

Like generations of Aberdonians before and since these folk are heading for the beach to enjoy themselves. This is the Spring Holiday, 1968.

Edwardian youngsters enjoying paddling at Aberdeen Beach.

Bathing machines, invented by Victorians to preserve the modesty of women sea bathers, cluster around the water's edge after having been towed there by donkeys like those seen on the left.

Victorians enjoying the sea air. A beach lifeboat can be seen. The fountain, complete with glass bowl in these days, is now at Hazlehead Park.

The Pleasure Beach in the early 1930s.

Enjoying themselves on the Aberdeen switchback railway.

Ready to set off on the helter-skelter ride of the impressive Aberdeen switchback.

Aberdeen's first switchback railway, an idea imported from America by showman Henry Duckworth. This stood on ground which is now North Esplanade West.

Fun for the children at the beach fairground in 1964.

Crowds at the carnival stalls at Aberdeen Beach in 1964.

Holiday fun at the Pleasure Beach in 1962.

Open-air dancing at Aberdeen Beach links in 1958.

The children's playground had plenty of customers on this sunny summer's day in 1965.

A horse and carriage ride along the beach promenade — a popular feature of the seaside entertainment for many years.

Unpredictable July weather couldn't deter this group of worshippers when the Church of Scotland seaside mission returned to Aberdeen Beach in 1965 after a gap of two years.

The beach mission in full song, July, 1969.

The Aberdeen beach shelter which was demolished in 1974 after many years as a landmark at the seafront.

Sheltering from the storm in the beach shelter, 1965.

The 'island' in the middle of the Beach Ballroom dance floor which many veteran dancegoers will remember.

The former restaurant at the Beach Ballroom.

A memento of when the public swimming pool was at Constitution Street.

The Bon-Accord Baths— or 'Uptown Baths' as they were popularly known — during construction which was from 1936 to 1940.

The Bon-Accord Ladies Pipe Band with the newly-formed dancers' section on their first public

An unusual view of the Bon-Accord Baths as workmen re-tile the pond in 1975. It was the first complete resurfacing since the 1940 opening.

engagement at Hazlehead Park in 1967.

The Belmont Club spins its roulette wheel for the first time on opening night, 1963.

Bon-Accord Silver Band gives an impromptu performance for families and friends before heading off for London and the National Brass Band Championship in 1968.

A sunny Sunday at Aberdeen Beach in 1961.

When the golden sands of Aberdeen ruled the holiday scene — 1932.

It's 1947 and the queue for deck chairs stretches into the distance.

Aberdeen schoolgirls enjoying themselves during a session of the BBC Radio One Club at the Palace Ballroom in 1970.

Ken Scott, leader of the resident band at the Palace Ballroom with the Bon-Accord Ladies Pipe Band during a special 'at home evening' in 1960.

Westburn Park is the place chosen by many to cool off during a 1959 heatwave.

All ready for the gala opening of the Palace Ballroom in 1960. The El Corisco coffee bar was a special feature of the refurbished dancehall. Music was by Ken Scott and his All Stars with vocalist Billie Campbell.

Fun for all at the Bay of Nigg, July 16, 1934.

Swimming instruction at the Middle School pond in 1962.

Bouffant hairdos and
coats at the 62 Club,
Summer Street, in
October, 1964.

The year is 1955 and
the slogan from
Aberdeen Town
Council's publicity
department for use in
the south is — the
Silver City with the
golden sands.

Westburn Park before the stream was widened.

A Gordon Highlanders' parade is the centre of attention with Aberdonians joining them as they march to the Cowdray Hall in 1930.

Dancing to the sounds of Syd Lawrence and his Orchestra at the Beach Ballroom in 1977.

Members of Aberdeen Repertory Theatre leave the Beach Pavilion after rehearsals in 1956. Third left is Walter Carr.

The St Bernard's Waltz at the Hazlehead outdoor dancing in 1972.

The pavilion at Hazlehead in the 1930s.

Enjoying the sun at Hazlehead in 1968.

Hula hoop star Linda Duffus of Newburgh gets seven hoops swinging in the junior heat of a competition at the then Regal Cinema in 1958.

More action from the hula hoop finals at The Regal in 1958.

It's the final number at the Hazlehead open-air dancing and at last there's some action on the dancing boards — July, 1965.

Gill Southcott shows a yo-yo can help you unwind at the Aberdeen Festival of 1975. Looking on are festival personalities Sandy Diack and John Mearns.

Syncopating Sandy
Strickland during his
157-hour non-stop
piano playing marathon
at Aberdeen Music Hall
in 1957.

Triumphant, but exhausted
Syncopating Sandy (with
hands bandaged)
is led through cheering
crowds. More than 36,000 paid
to see the 40-year-old Bolton
engineer play during his
record bid.

The North and Trinity Church when it was being converted into an adult education and civic arts centre in 1961.

The stage and auditorium of the Aberdeen Arts Centre in 1963.

The innovative Attic Players production of the musical *Cabaret* in 1978.

The Attic Theatre Group's pantomime of 1978 — *Sinbad the Sailor*. The Attic pantomimes became a well-loved part of Aberdeen's Festive season.

Two go-karts in action at Linksfield Stadium as the new form of racing is introduced to a fascinated North-East public in 1960.

About 1,200 North-East folk turned out for this go-kart racing demonstration in 1962 at Boyndie Aerodrome, near Banff.

Motor cycle racing at Cruden Bay, near Slains Castle, in 1950.

Aberdeen cyclist S.McRae takes the winning flag in the featherweight motor cycle championships at Cruden Bay in 1950.

Pittodrie overflowing in 1947 for a match against Hibs which holds the midweek record for attendance. The all-time record was in 1954 when 45,061 saw the Dons beat Hearts in a Scottish Cup fourth-round tie.

Bobby Simpson, captain of the victorious Sunnybank team, raises the Scottish Junior Cup in triumph in 1954.

Banks o' Dee muddied but victorious after the 1957 Scottish Junior Cup Final. Holding the cup is skipper Jimmy Warrender. Fourth left is goalkeeper Tubby Ogston who went on to a professional career with the Dons.

A goalmouth incident from Central Park in 1958 with the Lads' Club keeper under pressure from East End.

The Braemar Gathering in 1849 when it was held in front of Braemar Castle.

Braemar Gathering in 1921.

Spectators get an elevated view of the Braemar Gathering in 1949.

King George V arrives at the Braemar Gathering in 1924.

Queen Mary leads out the Royal party at Braemar in 1934.

King George VI and Queen Elizabeth arrive at Braemar by horse carriage in 1938.

Famous Games Heavy Bill Anderson of Bucksburn in action at Ballater.

The march of the clans to the Braemar Gathering in 1928. Here the Clan Duff crosses the Bridge of Cluny.

A 19th-century photograph of the Men of Lonach lined up in Tarland for an inspection by Queen Victoria

Dancers brave the weather at the Aboyne Highland Games in 1954.

Captain A.Forbes of the Scots Guards from Balmoral Castle winning the 1968 hill race at Ballater.

The Lonach Highlanders marching past the burned out shell of Candacraig House in 1955.

The restored Candacraig House makes a striking backdrop for the Men of Lonach during the 1967 march.

Duncan MacPherson, the oldest clansman of the time, addresses the Lonach Highlanders by megaphone in this photograph thought to be from 1929.

Banners flying, the Men of Lonach stride out during their five-mile Strathdon hike in 1969.

The Men of Lonach marching in the 1920s.

Competitors leaving the field during the famous hill race at the Ballater Games in 1969.

The View from Above

Aberdeen University Air Squadron fly over Marischal College with their new Bulldog aircraft in 1975. The Mitchell Tower and St Nicholas House are prominent below.

1964: Torry, the 'elder brother' of Aberdeen's south side communities, pressing into a bend of the River Dee (bottom left). The green circle known locally as 'The Moundie' is just visible top right.

Torry when it was still being developed.

The centre of Aberdeen in 1966 showing Union Terrace Gardens and the famous buildings around it.

A sunny day at Aberdeen Beach in 1966 with the chimney of the below-ground Beach Baths swimming pool prominent.

Trams, beach huts and bathing machines can be seen in this aerial photograph from the 1930s.

The Ashgrove housing estate (centre) starts to grow. The 'six roads' junction can be seen on the left.

Berryden, Westburn Park and Cornhill are in this aerial view from 1955.

Beechgrove House partially shrouded by trees is in the centre of this 1957 picture of Mile End.

The building of Northfield in 1949. Housing on Granitehill Road can be seen going up on the left of this view.

A 1950's picture of the harbour area, with Union Street on the left. Smoke from trains approaching and leaving Aberdeen Station is visible centre right.

A 1951 picture of an undeveloped Bridge of Don. Wartime defences still line the road to the beach.

Union Street — The Great Vision

WHEN over 100,000 people jammed into Union Street to celebrate its 200th anniversary on July 24, 1995, it was more than the biggest birthday party held in Europe. It was also a recognition of the special affection Aberdonians have for their greatest thoroughfare.

The date of the celebration provoked some debate. A project as massive as the building of Union Street has many birthdays. Mooted as early as 1790 it was in 1800 that the Town Council obtained Parliamentary powers to proceed and 1801 that work began.

The great Union Street plan was remarkable even for those confident times. Aberdeen was inspired by an ideal. A straight, wide street which would adorn the city and reflect its dignity and place of importance in the world.

Great vaults had to be constructed to level the many hills and hollows of the route, and a high bridge built over the Denburn. The 130-foot single span Union Bridge with its sculpted brass panels and fine views, became the star of the project creating a necessary break from the lofty granite buildings of the rest of the street.

It took many years before buildings stretched right along the street built on bridges. The high standards and elaborate styling the council insisted on scared many developers away. In fact the cost of Union Street bankrupted the burgh in 1817. It took eight years and the prosperity following the fall of Napoleon to sort out Aberdeen's finances, but even in those black days there was a refusal to lose sight of the original vision.

As you take a visual stroll down Union Street — and down through the years — in the following pages you may ask whether the councils of more recent times have stayed true to the spirit of their great inheritance.

Does Union Street continue to reflect the dignity of the city? Or is it degenerating into just another characterless main street? The sort you could find anywhere in the country.

In 1961 noted Aberdeen historian and architect Fenton Wyness wrote: 'The Union Street scheme took fully 60 years to complete but its degradation has been accomplished in a third of that time.' And Fenton was writing before the southern aspect of the Union Bridge was blotted out with shop units.

The Queen herself has commented on the decline of Union Street and hoped that better days lie ahead for it.

Union Street is today as much in need of men and women of vision and determination as it was 200 years ago. It should be remembered that when the council hesitated at the radical nature of the 'bridge street' plan it was the citizens who insisted on it going ahead — many putting large amounts of money into the project.

At the beginning of the 1880s a visitor to Aberdeen said that Union Street had 'the stability, cleanliness and architectural beauties of the London west-end streets.'

If visitors were to speak once again of Aberdeen's grandest street in such glowing terms that would be real cause for a celebration party in the year 2000, the true anniversary of the birth of Union Street.

The Holburn Street end of Union Street — a thoroughfare worthy of celebration.

The west end of Union Street in 1885 with horse drawn trams competing alongside traditional horse and carriage.

Union Street, devoid of motor cars – only trams, carts and cyclists to be seen.

No. 465 Union Street. It's 1971 and the For Sale signs are up on Marlowe's 'hairdresser's for ladies and gentlemen'. The red leather seats and courteous service of this superior hairdresser will be remembered by many.

At No. 492, one of the more impressive shops on the street — A & W Alexander, fishmonger, butchers and salesmen of game. Inside were large marble slabs and grandly carved wood. This was 1962.

Watt and Grant at No. 247. One of the city's best known stores with a national reputation and a special place in the affections of Aberdonians. The store closed in 1981, after 99 years of trading.

The Majestic Cinema in 1972.

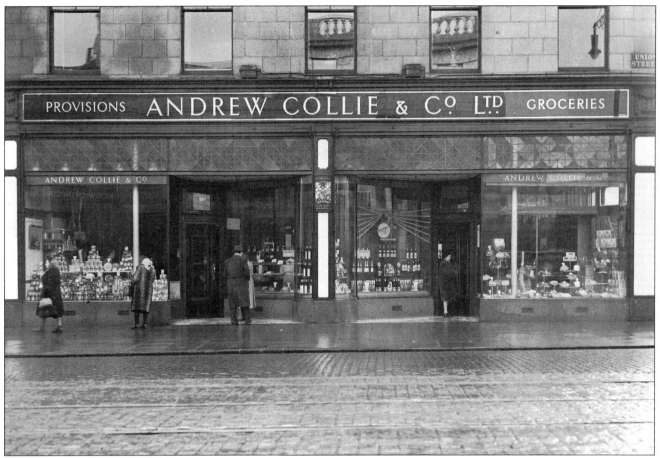

The wonderful aromas of coffees wafting from Andrew Collie & Co Ltd at 269 Union Street have entered the folklore of the city.

It's 1971 and the street is changing with the shutters up at Collies. Shirras Laing still have a shop nearby and the golden boot of Milne and Munro can also be seen.

No. 375 Union Street, showing the dignity and detail of the architecture.

The aftermath of the great December storm of 1908 with six-foot walls of snow on Union Street.

No. 150 Union
Street.

Kennaways restaurant,
Manfield the clothing
shop, and Marshall &
Philp selling kitchen
utensils, feature behind
this queue for the
Gaumont cinema.

Queuing for bananas at Peglers, No. 169 Union Street, in 1946 after wartime restrictions were lifted.

The classic view of 1900 looking west from the Union Bridge before fire destroyed the Palace Hotel *(left)*. The imposing Northern Assurance Company's building dominates the other side of the street.

The Palace Hotel in the 1930s. A 1941 blaze destroyed the building.

Union Street in all its grandeur in 1935.

A 1955 view with only a gap where the Palace Hotel once stood.

The store which children loved to visit to ogle the toys — McMillan's below the Trinity Hall in 1965.

The Union Bridge as its creators intended it to be seen.

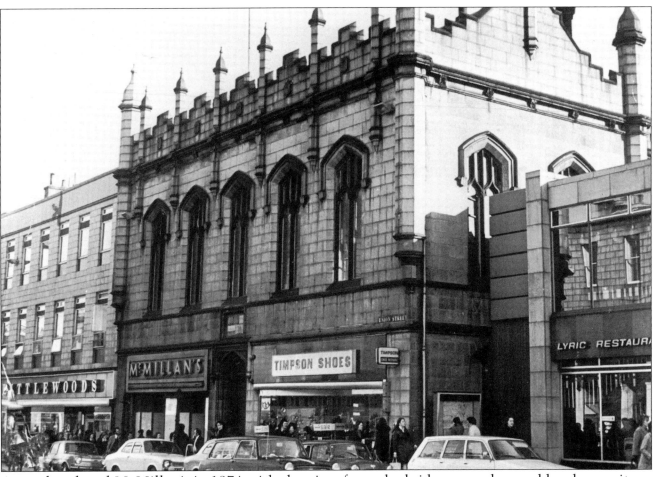

A much reduced McMillan's in 1974 with the view from the bridge now obscured by shop units.

Birrells and Goodsons in 1937. Littlewoods now stands on this site.

A bleak wartime night on Union Street with the few lights glistening on the cassies.

F.W.Woolworths '3d and 6d store'— the first of its kind in the city.

Previous page, top: It's 1959 and
Woolworth has adapted to the needs
of a new generation, their slogan
'nothing over sixpence' long since
discarded.

Previous page, bottom: A
thunderstorm all but clears the
street in 1957.

It's 1960 and some weel kent names are under threat from plans by property developers — Raffan,
R. J. Smith and Leslie Hatt.

The Falconers store is to the fore in this 1950s view of the final stretch of Union Street.

The east end of Union Street with the 'new' Town House clock and tower of 1871 prominent.

Looking west from the Castlegate in 1942 after a January snowstorm.

Horse and cart power helps clear the snow away beside Broad Street.

No. 15 Union Street as it looked in the early 1930s.

Looking back along Union Street in February 1952 as massive crowds gather to hear the Accession Declaration of Elizabeth II following the death of her father.

City of Change

The Gordon Highlanders on parade in Castlehill Barracks.

General Sir Ian Hamilton inspects the Gordons at Castlehill Barracks in 1934.

The historic scene as the Gordons march from Castlehill Barracks for the last time in August, 1935.

The flats at Castlehill Barracks in 1958.

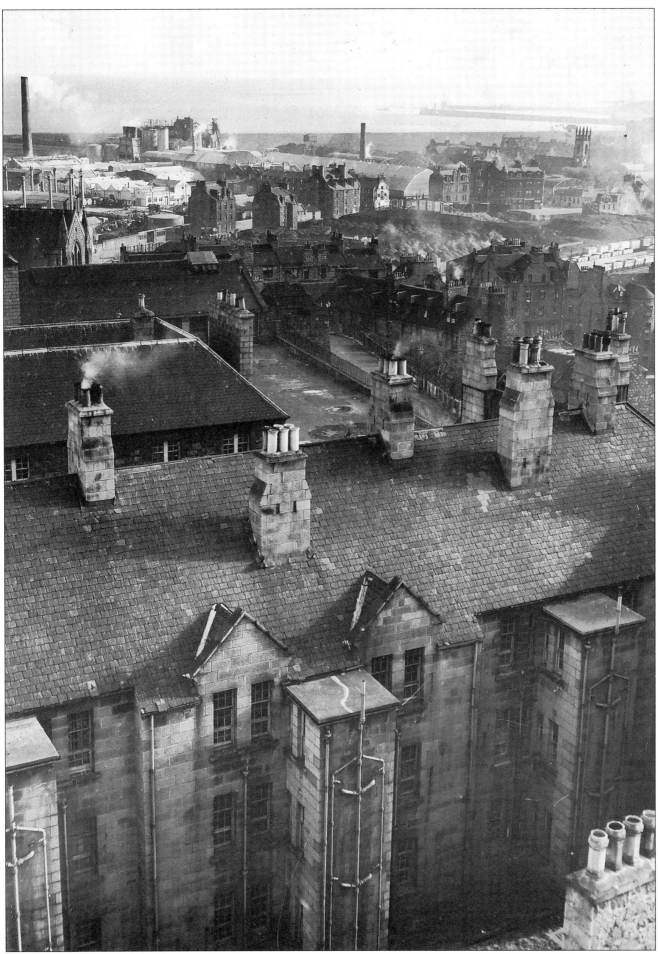

A view of the Castlehill Barracks site in 1959.

Castlehill Barracks — the site of a garrison from 1794 — is demolished in 1960.

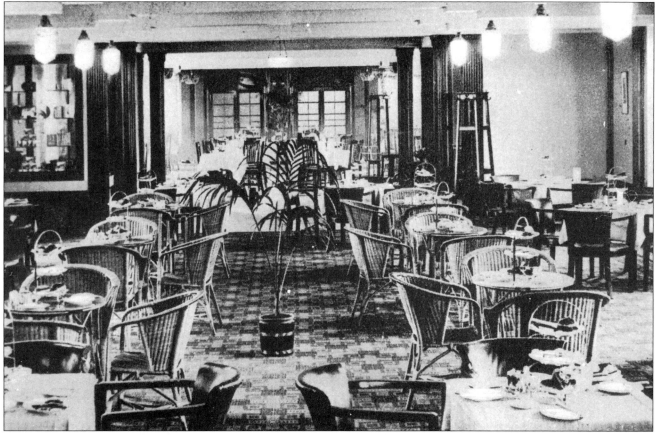

Famous Aberdeen store Isaac Benzie's which set up business in 1894 and opened their department store at 143-167 George Street in the early 1930s. This is the second-floor restaurant and tea room where the Lambeth Wilson Trio played.

Watt and Grant, on the corner of Crown Street and Dee Village Road, decked out in celebration and proudly proclaiming themselves silk mercers and furriers.

G. M. Smith, newsagent and general merchant on Crown Street and Village Road. A study from the age of aspidistras (see windows above shop) and gaslight.

Morrison's Economic Stores on St Nicholas Street. Jimmy Mearns made this store a North-East institution with bulk buying and a shrewd appreciation of what the public wanted.

It's the same site as Morrison's, but in 1964 it's another shopping institution which is trading in the Netherkirkgate ... and preparing for a big expansion.

Reid & Pearson on St
Nicholas Street in 1965
— celebrating their
diamond jubilee.

The North Co-op's
arcade in Loch
Street decked out for
Christmas 1969.

The site about to house the rapidly expanding Bridge of Don's first bank in 1973.

Sunnyview Tenements, Mastrick, in 1955.

The site where the Aberdeen Journals building stood in Broad Street. This picture was taken just after the demolition in 1973.

Crowds gather at the Tarry Bridge on St Clement's Street for a special ceremony believed to be the opening. A line of buses is crossing over.

A glimpse of the main entrance to Advocates Hall from an archway in Concert Court which takes its name from the concerts held there in the 18th century.

A prison for Aberdeen. Craiginches is constructed in 1891 to house child abusers and drunkards.

The old and the new in Mastrick, 1955. An ageing wash house and lavatory in the foreground with modern Upper Mastrick Way houses in the background.

Aberdeen's first high flats block rises in March, 1960.

The Ashgrove flats are completed and long queues form to view Aberdeen's new skyscraper in March, 1961.

Ashgrove flats and the work going on around in April, 1961.

The £70,000 Auchinyell Road bridge nears completion in February, 1961.

The approach to the Brig o' Balgownie in 1938, showing rows of houses soon to be demolished.

A boating scene at the Brig o' Balgownie from the early 1890s.

Alternative spellings at Baltic Street in 1944.

Preparing to build the
Beach Boulevard in 1957.

An early picture of
Beechgrove House, which
later became the BBC
headquarters in Aberdeen
and home of the Beechgrove
Garden television
programme.

The Friday Market at the Castlegate in 1930.

New housing going up at Balnagask in 1969.

The Bridge of Dee from Ruthrieston School in 1959.

An 1892 view of Bridge Street.

The Winter Gardens at the Duthie Park in 1972.

Traffic negotiates the narrow Bridge of Don in 1952.

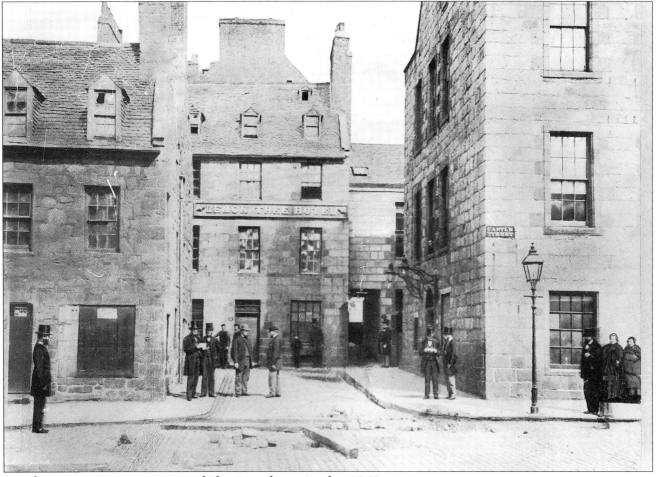

Castle Street, Huxter Row and the Broadgate in the 1860s.

A print from a glass slide showing Rolland's Lodgings in the Castlegate.

Rolland's Lodgings takes on a different appearance before it was bought and run by the Poor Association. A landmark for 300 years it was finally demolished in 1935.

The Castlegate in the 1930s.

Shoes, clothes and pots and pans for sale at one of the Castlegate's famous markets.

Muckle Friday at the Castlegate where farmers hired workers for the coming season on this ancient market day.

It's 1936 and this is the last night for the Castlegate coffee stall. City magistrates refused to renew its lease. The neatly-groomed staff were an institution, serving hot drinks, sweets and cigarettes into the small hours.

The Albion Street Congregational Church which was due to be demolished soon after this picture was taken in the 1930s.

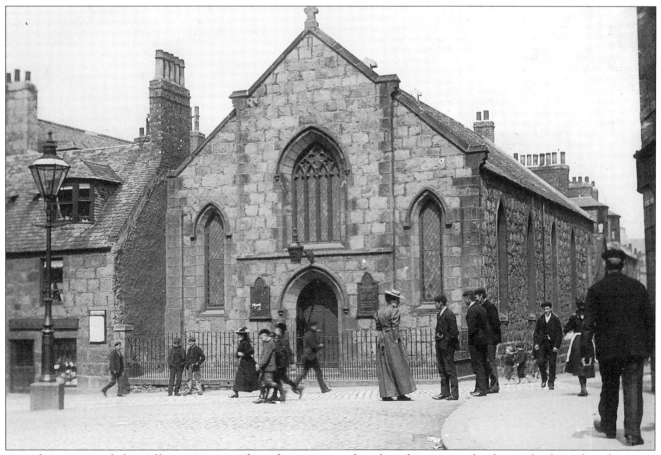

Another view of the Albion Street Church, a centre for the charities which worked in the slums.

A 1937 picture
of the very
narrow
Thomas Place,
Old Aberdeen.

The Mounthooly-
Causewayend
junction pictured in
1932.

Council officials take a census of traffic in the narrow Netherkirkgate in 1957.

Cheyne's the motor cycle dealers on the corner of Holburn Street and Willowbank Road in 1960.

The toppling of Morton's chimney in 1938 draws a big crowd in the background.

Nelson Lane, a photograph from 1936.

An historic picture of Queen's Cross when it was virtually in the countryside.

Cumberland House as Provost Skene's House was known because of a brief stay by The Duke of Cumberland.

Sir George Skene's House in the Guestrow was the town house of this noted family.

Peacock's Close in 1953.

The housing which used to surround King's College, Old Aberdeen.

Reid's Place which is understood to have once been in the Shiprow area.

The Public Library, St Mark's Church (formerly the South United Free Church), and the Wallace Statue, but His Majesty's Theatre is still to be built. This study is from 1902. The theatre was built in 1906 and a new reading room added to the library in 1905.

A study of Short Loanings printed from a lantern plate by Aberdeen Camera Club founder Alexander MacKilligan in 1910.

A mother and toddler at the corner of Shoe Lane in the 1930s.

Denburn Road in 1957 with the Union Bridge in the distance still free of shops.

Trees being cut down at Rubislaw Terrace Gardens in 1960.

The junction of St Nicholas Street and Schoolhill with a policeman on point duty in 1959.

Queuing for petrol at Union Grove Motors in 1964.

The approach to the Spital in 1968 showing Auckland Place on the right.

The Snug Bar on Virginia Street in 1965.

Shuttle Lane looking towards East North Street. This picture was taken in the late 1930s before families were moved to new housing estates.

Washday in an Aberdeen slum area in the 1930s.

Spring Gardens in the 1930s before some of the buildings on the right were demolished.

Unveiling the King Edward VII statue on October 28, 1914. A 20,000 crowd braved rain and wind, and an hour's delay, to see the unveiling ceremony.

The Town and County Garage at 19 Justice Mill Lane in the 1930s.

Portal Crescent, Tillydrone, at its junction with Wingate Road in 1958.

Albyn Place during the war years with blackout markings on walls and posts to aid drivers.

Union Terrace Gardens at the turn of the century.

Union Terrace Gardens, prior to 1906 when His Majesty's Theatre was built.

The booking office of Schoolhill Station which became a café and was demolished in the 1970s.

The Cowdray Hall nears completion.

The Upperkirkgate in 1953.

Young Street looking towards the Gallowgate where the Technical College now stands.

The historic Longacre area.

Another view of the Longacre, standing close to Marischal College.

A view of Torry taken from across the river in 1967.

Traffic on Victoria Bridge, Torry, in 1965.

Sinclair Road, Torry, at the turn of the century.

The view from Kincorth in 1934.

The fields set to become the Kincorth housing estate.

A 1934 view of the Kincorth area about to become filled with homes.

Yet another view from Kincorth in 1934.

Old Torry in 1936.

An historic
photograph of Torry
dock.

Another photograph of Torry dock in Edwardian times.

The Torry Battery around 1935 with fishing nets laid out in the foreground.

The ferry at Bieldside in 1955 with ice flows from the Dee strewn by the path.

The wartime rocket site at the Links, still there in the 1950s when this picture was taken.

Birth of an Airport

Eric Gandar Dower, father of Aberdeen Airport, welcomes Prime Minister Ramsay MacDonald to Dyce Aerodrome on July 11, 1934.

Gandar Dower *(centre)* and Lord Arbuthnott *(left)* at the official opening of the aerodrome at Dyce on July 28, 1934.

Aviation pioneer Eric Gandar Dower at the controls of a De Havilland Rapide which flew on the route from Aberdeen to Wick, Orkney and Shetland.

Another milestone in the history of Aberdeen aviation as Gandar Dower *(second right)* and Aberdeen council officials pause for a picture before the first commercial flight to Stavanger in the late 1930s.

Electioneering in 1945. Gandar Dower ready to set off and spread his message.

The original terminal building at Aberdeen Airport which Eric Gandar Dower used for his Allied Airways passengers is seen beside the newer terminal in 1972.

Planning the way ahead at the airport — Gandar Dower and one of his captains.

A Viscount refuelling at the tiny Dyce Airport of 1956.

Aberdeen Airport, Dyce, in 1975 is flourishing with passenger numbers up from 129,700 in 1969 to 450,000. A new £7 million terminal is planned.

Aberdeen Aerodrome and the surrounding fields at Dyce in 1949 when there were 1,942 departures on scheduled flights.

The original hangar at Dyce in the 1930s.

The Haugh of Dyce with the village in the foreground before the air age arrived in 1934. Very prominent are skating and curling ponds which were opened in 1890.

The crew of a Blenheim bomber and their plane at Dyce in 1942. The RAF had a base at the airport from 1937 to 1957.

Passengers on their way to the planes from the Aberdeen Airport reception area in 1969.

By 1976 Aberdeen Airport had one of the busiest heliports in the world and could accommodate almost all jets apart from Jumbos.

Land and Sea

The farming industry which contributed so much to Aberdeen's growth is seen here in 1966 with housing beginning to encroach on the fields.

Tattie holidays were an established part of the North-East scene until very recently, and even town loons were found taking part in the back-aching work.

A ploughing match at Cults when Lower Deeside was an agricultural area rather than part of Aberdeen's urban sprawl. The women are described as 'Keith and Cairnie, lady ploughing champions'.

How the harvest was gathered in 1937 showing stooks being prepared.

The Aberdeen port entrance, Old Torry and Footdee about 1902.

The city from the harbour in 1890. The Town House clock tower is a prominent landmark on the skyline.

Aberdeen Harbour was also busy and bustling in Victorian times.

A harbour scene from the steam age, around 1925. The graceful *St Sunniva* of that time can be seen at her cross berth. This ship foundered in dense fog in the 1930s.

The Weigh House, which stood where the harbour offices now are.

A quayside scene at the busy Point Law in 1888.

A Torry fishwife from the turn of the century.

Fishwives off to fill their baskets with silver darlings at the start of the herring season in 1937.

Loading herring on to an Aberdeen herring curers' vehicle in the 1930s.

Aberdeen 'sputnik' class trawlers at Torry Dock in 1965.

No threat from this U-boat which attracted sightseers to Aberdeen Harbour, August, 1945.

Unloading a ship in Aberdeen Harbour in the steam age.

Gordon Highlanders boarding the *St Rognvald* in August, 1939, possibly to sail to Scapa Flow.

The Aberdeen motor powered lifeboat of 1937.

The Aberdeen lifeboat of 1948 in action.

The Aberdeen lifeboat *Hilton Briggs* draws the crowds in 1951.

The old Aberdeen lifeboat at the Christening ceremony for the new lifeboat on the River Dee in 1952.

Aberdeen's latest lifeboat, *BP Forties,* is followed by the conventional lifeboat *Ramsay Dyce* and escort vessels as it is introduced to the public in 1976.

Days of Toil

The men — and woman — who ran the Co-operative Society's horse-drawn delivery service in the early 1940s. This picture was taken at the Co-op's meal mill at Berryden. *Evening Express* reader John Foote, who supplied this photograph, worked as a Saturday boy when there were 80 horses for the grocery department, 100 for the milk rounds and 40 for the bakery department.

The sturdy men of the Shore Porters removal service. The company, which was founded in 1498, was said to favour employing strapping country loons.

The girls of Ogston & Tennant's soap factory.

The production line at John Robertson (canisters) Ltd, Roslin Place, Aberdeen, in 1966. The women are producing gallon tins for paint and oil.

The Bon-Accord Distillery in the Hardgate which had a capacity of more than 300,000 proof gallons a year seen around 1900. A spectacular fire destroyed most of it.

The interior of Duncan Fraser, draper, in 1962.

The 1911 delivery fleet of the Shore Porters seen here in King Street.

Duncan Fraser, the drapery shop which was established in 1912.

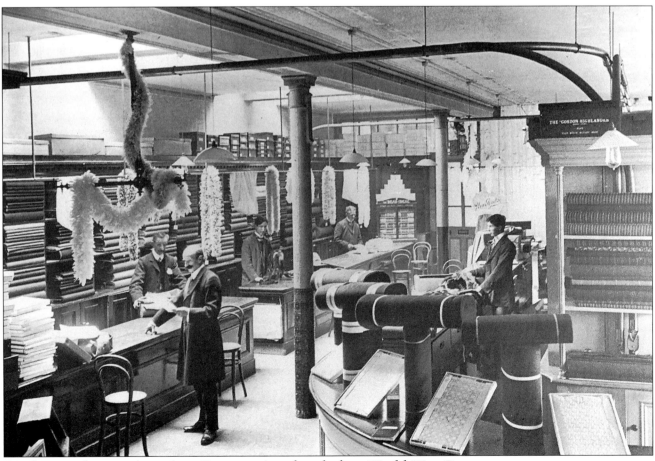

Frock-coated supervisors in a Co-operative shop before World War One.

The Northern Co-operative Society drapery shop in 1961.

The old and new methods of transport for delivering milk seen here in 1950.

The Aberdeen Blind Asylum in 1959 with men at work weaving baskets.

At work on chairs in the Aberdeen Blind Asylum of 1952.

A tar laying machine at work on Union Grove in 1952.

The fleet of Alexander's vans outside the new-look showroom in Holburn Street in 1958.

Salmon fishers at work tending their nets at the bothy by the River Dee on Riverside Drive in 1936.

A giant block of granite on the floor of Rubislaw Quarry is measured by two workers in 1964.

A 1956 study of the Aberdeen Coal and Shipping Co. at work.

The new Mini has pride of place in the showroom window in this picture from the 1960s.

Night City Taxi's driver Bert Leitch takes a call while at work in 1957.

The first Aberdeen Panda Patrol on parade in October, 1968.

Dramas

Firemen pour water on the blazing Isaac Spencer oil and paint warehouse at Albert Quay in 1960.

Sixty firemen fought the blaze on the evening of July 8, 1960, which destroyed most of the Isaac Spencer paint warehouse.

The north islands ferry is allowed through the fishermen's blockade of Aberdeen Harbour in 1975 during three days of national action over foreign fish imports.

The blockade is secure again, totally closing the harbour.

The flood-swollen River Dee submerges Riverside Drive in 1951.

Rescuers toil under the glare of arc lights after the collapse of the Zoology Building in 1966.

Climber Robert Burnett, who was brought back alive after being buried by snow in an avalanche in the Cairngorms, January, 1964, gets an injection as he lies on the tractor bogie used to carry him down from the mountains.

Mountaineers taking part in the operation to find five hillwalkers who were caught in storms travelling from Braemar to Glen Dollon, New Year, 1959. All five died.

Special Visitors

The one-year-old Princess Elizabeth is intrigued by a photographer as she is pushed by her nurse with Queen Mary, the Duchess of York, King George V and the Duke of York following at a 1927 Balmoral fete.

Princess Elizabeth and Princess Margaret create great interest as they arrive at Ballater Station in 1932 at the start of another Deeside holiday.

A birthday party at Elsick House in 1935. From left, the then Duchess of York, Lord and Lady Carnegie. The children are Princess Elizabeth, Zoe d'Erlanger, Mary Anna Sturt, Princess Margaret, Master Wolrige Gordon and the Master of Carnegie.

Happy family scene at the Braemar Gathering with the little Princesses and their parents.

Princess Elizabeth at a King's Camp at Abergeldie in 1939. Also sharing the joke are Princess Margaret and Queen Elizabeth.

In 1946 the two Princesses had the poise of confident young women when they arrived at Ballater Station from Aberdeen.

Princess Elizabeth at the Aboyne Ball in 1949.

Princess Elizabeth with Prince Charles and Nurse Lightbody with the month-old Princess Anne in 1950 at Aberdeen station.

Princess Elizabeth and
Princess Margaret on the
Royal Train at Aberdeen.
Just a few months later,
in February 1952,
Princess Elizabeth
ascended to the throne.

The Queen serves
customers at the
Crathie Church sale of
work in 1955.

June 2, 1953, and huge crowds flood Union Street to see the Coronation procession of Queen Elizabeth

with Queen Victoria surveying the scene from the corner of St Nicholas Street.

The Queen enjoying an autumn day on the Deeside moors in 1967.

Bottom, left: Prince Andrew and Viscount Linley arrive at Ballater, complete with corgis.

Bottom, right: Prince Andrew and Prince Edward at Aberdeen Harbour in 1972.

The Queen returns to travelling by train to Aberdeen in 1975 after a few years of arriving at the start of her Deeside holiday on the Royal Yacht *Britannia*.

A reluctant corgi is encouraged to follow the Queen on to the train at Aberdeen in 1978.

Caring for the Citizens

The grim facade of the Royal Aberdeen Hospital for Sick Children at Castlehill. The hospital was founded in 1877.

A nurse and child on the stone stairs leading to one of the corridors in the Castlehill building known as the 'Sick Kids'.

The rear view of the 'Sick Kids' at Castlehill.

The Sick Children's Hospital before it became the Royal Aberdeen Children's Hospital and moved to Foresterhill in 1929.

A 1960 advance in caring for the new-born — an incubator to keep babies at the correct temperature.

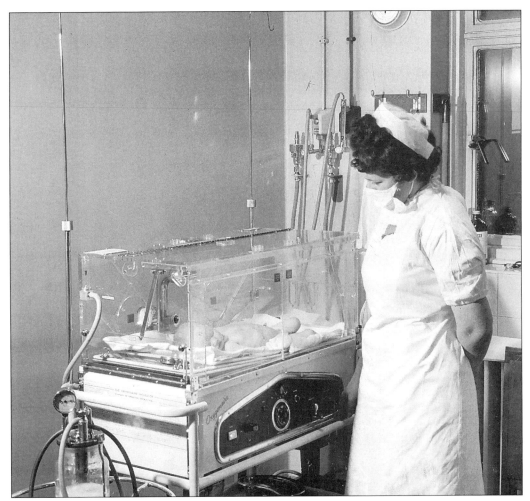

The Sick Children's Hospital at Castle Terrace in the 1920s when the only way to escape from stifling wards was by moving on to narrow balconies.

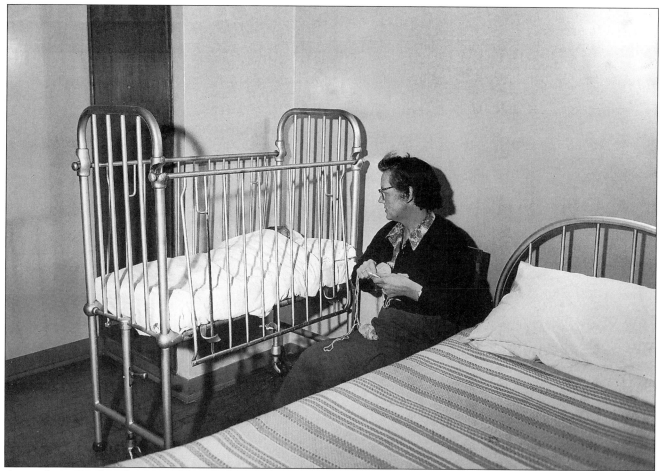

A mother sits by the cot of her baby at the Mother-and-Baby Unit at Foresterhill. The year is 1960.

A ward at Aberdeen Royal Infirmary, Woolmanhill, around 1900.

Everyone helps out serving food at the Torry Nursery in the 1940s.

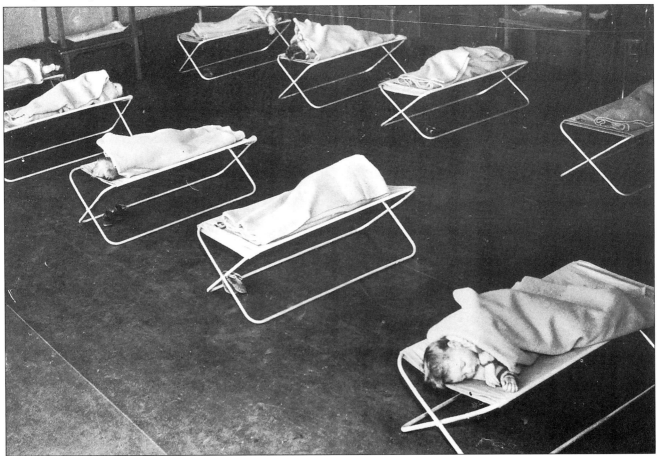

Bedtime for youngsters of yesteryear at Torry Nursery where they had a compulsory hour's sleep through the day.

Subscribers

M Adamson

William J D Anderson

Kevin Angus

Margaret Catherine Argo

J Ross Baird

Mr W Bick

Raymond Black

Donald Brilz

Gordon E Bruce

Thomas R Burman

Mr Stanley Buyers

W & K Buyers

Sheila M Campbell

Susan Caroline

W Christie

Alex Clark

John A Clark

Richard H Clark

Walton S Cole (USA)

Miss Betty E Cooper

Mr Charles Coutts

Mr R C B Cowling

David Cruickshank

Mrs Violet Cruickshank

Frank L Deans

Jim Dent

Anne M Donald

Margaret Donald

David Dunbar

Mrs Joan Duncan

Mr John Duthie

Joyce Everill

W A Faerestrand

Mr & Mrs Fairbairn

George & Mary Findlay

Ian Findlay

Margaret & Bert Findlay

Lisa B Finnie

Angus C Forbes

Ayleen Mary Fraser

Billy Fraser

Ronald Fraser

Dennis Frew

Sheila W Gall

Catherine Gilchrist

John Giles

A C Gordon

Alasdair B Gordon

Phyllis Gordon

Amy Grant

Adam Gray

David G Gray

Arthur Grieve

David Hay

Mrs Sheila Hay

Gladys Henry

Joanne Lee Hogan

Ian Hogg

Michael Johnston

Mr & Mrs A Keith

John Keith

Graham Kerr

Jacqueline D Leith

R G Lowe

Mr Henry M Lumsden

George Lee Lynch

Jim Rose

Mr Ian Rowatt

Mr Tommy Russell

Alex Ryrie

Mr Donald Shaw

Mrs Isabella Shaw

Peter G Shearer

Moira E Shepherd

Brian Simpson

Ian B M & Dolina M Skinner

Dorothy Smith

Mr G G Smith

Norman & Helen Smith

Robert Smith

Douglas L Soppitt

Mr Dennis G Stephen

Jim & Jean Stott (Canada)

John Stuart

Allison & Ian Taylor

Miss J Taylor

Robert Taylor

Shirley Thomson

Derek Watson

Mr John Watson

John McMilllan Watt JP

Joseph Watt

Valerie Webster

George Westland

C Wight

M Wilson

Archie Wiseman

Rachel Macaskill Lorimer Yorston

James Young